how can we be a great team?

# Share

## Share booklet 07

This *Share booklet* is one of a series which aims to encourage discussion about fresh expressions of church, without telling you what to do.

01 how can fresh expressions emerge?

02 how should we start?

03 what should we start?

04 how can we get support?

05 how can we find our way?

06 how can we be sustainable?

**07 how can we be a great team?**

## Contents

| | |
|---|---|
| Hitting the right note | 3 |
| Forming | 4 |
| Norming | 6 |
| Storming | 8 |
| Performing | 12 |
| Adjourning | 14 |

# Hitting the right note

*How can we be a great team?* is about the vital importance of nurturing the team (or missional community) throughout a fresh expression's life.

## Shaping the future

This booklet does not offer you a step-by-step model but explores how the missional community - whether large or small - enables the new church to emerge and sets its tone.

Research shows that in the business world teams of entrepreneurs rather than any one person found a substantial proportion, perhaps the majority, of new ventures.

## A framework

Here is a well-established framework to explore some of the issues involved but puts the topics in a slightly different order than normal:

- forming;
- norming;
- storming;
- performing;
- adjourning.

These are not so much distinct stages as overlapping and often parallel aspects of a missional community's life. Each aspect is likely to be present in one way or other throughout the group's existence.

# Forming

Forming the missional community will occur throughout the community's life as members join and leave. Forming involves members getting to know each other and establishing ground rules. It is about forming the community's identity. When you start hearing 'we' rather than 'I', you will know this process is well underway.

## Getting to know you

Forming includes welcoming new members. Willing helpers may not be readily at hand, so realistic expectations are necessary. Keep the following in mind:

- **additions to the group have down as well as upsides.**

    Unless they are replacing someone, a new member will make the missional community larger and perhaps more complex. Leading it could become more demanding.

- **a more diverse group can improve the community's capacity.**

    The team will have a wider range of skills and networks. More diverse views can produce better decisions. But diversity may also reduce cohesion, increase conflict and cause an actual decline in effectiveness. The 'exchange theory' of groups maintains that individuals want to get out of a group at least as much as they put in. Balancing these considerations needs prayerful thought.

- **size may affect the time it takes the community to form.**

Forming should be about forming community, even if there are just two of you. If the missional community sets the tone for the fresh expression and community is essential to being church, then community must be at the heart of the team's life.

Teams with a community feel have an emphasis on horizontal relationships. Individuals don't just relate to the leader, they have strong ties to others in the team. There is a sense of shared decision-making and mutual support. Taking deliberate steps to get to know one another will start to create community. These might include doing things together, such as giving a meal together or going away for a day.

Warm-up exercises can encourage the sharing of experiences or stories. Doing a Myers-Briggs or Belbin Team Roles exercise will reveal members' gifts and deepen the team's sense of community.

> Garry Poole
> *The Complete Book of Questions: 1001 Conversation Starters for any Occasion*
> Zondervan, 2003

Encouraging individuals to share their lives is vital. Jesus and the disciples had close fellowship, as did members of the early church. The leader will play a key role by modelling openness: Jesus did not hide that he struggled in the Garden of Gethsemane - that's how we know! When leaders show they are incomplete, they open the door for others to help.

# Reconnect

# Story

Welcoming new members to help form missional community has been part and parcel of Reconnect's life since it came into being in Poole. As a newly-licensed pioneer minister in September 2008, Paul Bradbury set the ball rolling by renting an office in a café and then being quite disciplined about not 'doing' anything. For six months he and his wife Emily prayed, prayer walked, listened to what local residents were saying, chatted to those who knew the area and got a sense of what God was doing.

People were soon drawn to become part of the community because of its focus on making real friends with people - not just to tell them about the Gospel and the love of God but actually to get to know them and really to try and meet their needs in all kinds of physical ways as well as spiritual.

They found that forming community takes time. Other voices tried to tempt them to run an off the shelf programmatic approach to evangelism or mission but the recognition that relationship has to be built - and roots established - meant that it could not be rushed.

'Use the gifts that you've got' was a message that came through very strongly to them. This was demonstrated when a common interest in felt making brought together two people in a small group of 10 to start running felt making workshops. These sessions in turn developed into a monthly felt making group.

When later commissioned as a community, Reconnect members signed a rule of life - developed by looking at Acts and the gospels to find out what it means to be a community of disciples. As time went on, other initiatives began to emerge and Reconnect is now part of the Poole Missional Communities charity - set up to oversee and support the town's pioneering Christian work and protect the growing community's identity.

Reconnect's vision is to multiply the numbers of people who are opening their homes, engaging with those around them, using their gifts and talents - and working together to ensure a community that has Jesus at its core.

# Norming

Norming (establishing shared values) occurs as members work together, developing close relationships of trust. It involves negotiating roles, relationships and task procedures. As such, it overlaps with 'forming'.

## Share and share alike

This phase is complete when members accept a common set of expectations about how to do things. But the process may restart when a significant new member joins or a significant transition occurs in the fresh expression's life.

Spiritual norms should be nurtured as a priority. They will centre on members' inner hearts. Addressing the inner heart includes clearing it of barriers to healthy relationships.

This clearing process, which is ongoing, is a work of the Spirit. The Spirit of Christ, who self-emptied himself to the extreme of death, cleanses the inner heart of its preoccupation with self. Prayer and other spiritual practices are used by the Spirit to do this. Clearing a path for the Spirit within the team is ultimately the leader's responsibility, but might the team appoint a 'spiritual guide' for this purpose?

> *expressions: making a difference* 
> Fresh Expressions, 2011 
> Chapter 26: Tubestation
>
> The original pioneers at Tubestation felt the need to appoint a spiritual director as the community developed.

Encouraging 'communal' norms is also essential and involves going the extra mile for others in the team. Members care for each other, which enhances team working by:

- **developing trust;**

  Individuals will be more likely to express emotions and accept the emotional expressions of others. This fosters open communications, which expands members' knowledge of others' motivations, goals and viewpoints and lessens misunderstandings that can undermine trust.

- **increasing identification;**

  Individuals understand each other better and so begin to see others' perspectives, resources and identities as extensions of their own.

- **strengthening the sense of mutual obligation**

  'One good turn deserves another'. Empathising with others increases the willingness to help. The team works better.

It is important, therefore, that the group keeps working at these 'communal' practices and does not take them for granted. Getting to know one another and sharing each others' lives should be part of norming, as well as forming.

Encouraging 'task' norms involves developing very simple understandings of how members will work together - from how often the team meets to what will happen during the meetings, such as the use of milestone reviews. See Share → *How can we find our way? (Share booklet 05).*

> Michael Moynagh, Andy Freeman
> *Share: How can we find our way*
> (05)
> Fresh Expressions, 2011
>
> Book

How task-focused norms (which emerge as the work proceeds) become accepted helps to shape the community's life. For instance:

- **are norms set by the leader or agreed by the group as a whole?**

    The more that norms are owned by the group, the greater will be members' commitment to it.

- **how effectively are norms 'defended' by community members?**

    Norms that are upheld bring a degree of certainty and predictability to the group, which alleviates anxiety - especially helpful in pioneering contexts of uncertainty.

- **are norms intentionally reviewed from time to time?**

    For example, by periodically inviting members to comment on their ways of working and suggest improvements? Bringing to light difficulties will increase members' ownership of working arrangements.

Without 'the second mile' of communal norms, task-centred relationships can become mechanical, over-formal and rigid, with a loss of creativity. But a communal emphasis without appropriate task norms can produce an ill-disciplined team that fails to achieve its goals.

Communal and task norms, undergirded by self-emptying hearts, will build trust, group identity and mutual obligation. When team members face uncertainty and disappointment, their norms of working together will see them through.

# Storming

Storming is usually put after forming, because there can be an uncomfortable period of jostling between members before the group settles down. But we list it third, at the centre of the five aspects of a missional community's life, to symbolise the central part that storming (or conflict) can be expected to play.

## Agree to disagree

It helps to have realistic expectations. Conflict is natural in a healthy team. Think of all the disagreements among the disciples and in the early church!

Conflict:

- **may reflect the pioneering nature of the task.**

    Because the group is engaged in something new, it cannot always rely on previous knowledge. The resulting uncertainty and confusion may produce conflict, heightened by anxiety.

- **may reflect a healthy diversity within the group.**

    Different viewpoints allow issues to be considered from a variety of angles. Something important is less likely to be overlooked.

- **can be a sign that individuals are being given space - that no one is being suppressed.**

    Healthy communities may even encourage dissent to enable their members to flourish. Conflict can indicate that power in the group is dispersed.

- **can help to build community.**

    As team members share their real thoughts and feelings, endure the hurt of disagreement and find that they still accept each other at the end. Conflicts are the growing pains of community.

- **can provide good learning if handled constructively.**

    A new church that copes well with conflict will show how to use conflict fruitfully in other situations, which will be a blessing to society.

For these reasons, conflict should be welcomed when handled well. This positive attitude will reduce anxiety and give members greater confidence to face their disagreements. Agreed practices for handling disagreements may be helpful, negotiated as part of the norming process.

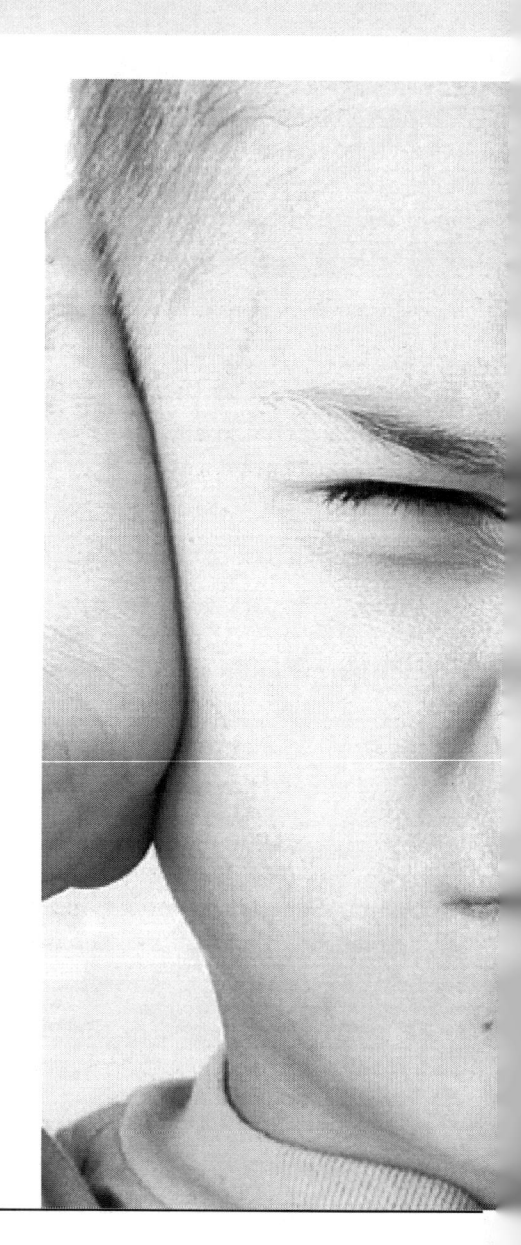

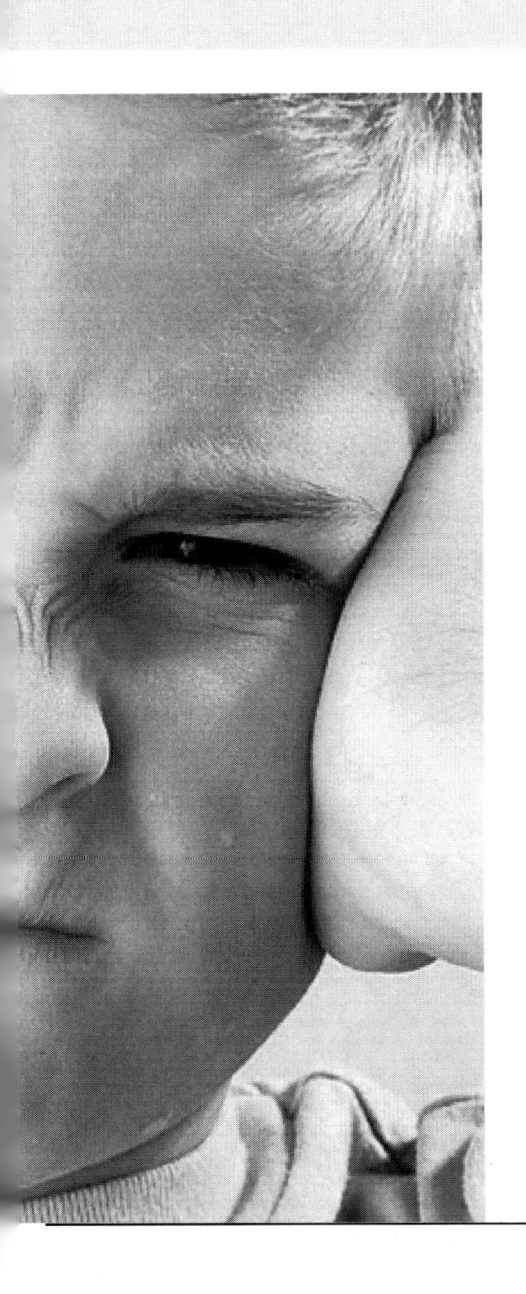

One youth church spent two evenings talking about how best to handle conflict. The teenagers came up with a host of ideas. These were distilled into some key principles, such as sort things out immediately and don't talk about others behind their backs.

A key leadership role is to articulate differences. When group members disagree, it is important that the leader keeps re-expressing the various views. The leader should do this whether or not they are chairing the meeting, and especially if they are a protagonist in the debate. Articulating the different views:

- **shows the parties that they have been understood, reducing anxiety.**

    Demonstrating that individuals have been heard is one of the few tasks the leader cannot delegate.

- **helps the parties understand each other.**

    Hearing the same point in different words can bring clarity, while hearing it expressed calmly can encourage a rational instead of an emotional response. The leader may comment that a view is strongly held, but conveying that information in an emotionally detached way will encourage greater detachment by others. Individuals are encouraged to process the group's feelings without being swamped by them.

- **allows contributions to be reframed so as to bring people together.**

    Comments can be re-expressed in a way others may understand. Especially when disagreements disrupt the group, might an outside facilitator help?

A time of quiet can give space for individuals to reconnect with the Spirit, distance themselves a little from the issues and get a wider perspective. They can be encouraged to pay attention to their inner hearts. What are they feeling strongly about? Why? Are there motives that should be taken to the cross?

Conflict is best managed within communities of grace. In 'grace-full' missional communities, members recognise their own flaws, weaknesses and need of forgiveness, making them more ready to forgive others. Forgiveness smothers resentment and enables conflict to be handled constructively.

How conflict is managed will do much to shape a team. If members learn to handle conflict constructively:

- **the missional community will feel safe;**
- **levels of honesty will rise;**
  This will strengthen community and aid performance.
- **a more diverse membership will be possible;**
  This will broaden the gifts, insights and network connections available to the community.
- **power is likely to be distributed more widely within the group.**

> *expressions: making a difference*
> Fresh Expressions, 2011
> Chapter 24: The Wesley Playhouse
> 
> At The Wesley Playhouse, converting a building for missional use was controversial but is now fully supported by the original congregation.
>
> DVD

As the missional community evolves, with members joining and leaving, the leader would be wise occasionally to review their leadership style. If this can done openly with the team, what a sign of maturity!

# Tubestation

# Story

In 2006, a Methodist chapel overlooking a beach in north Cornwall decided to redesign its premises in a bid to make it more accessible to the surfers who flocked to the area all year round. Tubestation was the result.

The chapel building, transformed into a surf lounge internet café, also boasts facilities such as indoor skate ramps. It attracts high expectations from visitors but its leaders say everything hinges on the concept of love your neighbour.

As that concept has taken root in Polzeath, discipleship - both in small groups and with individuals - is on the increase. Trust is also being built up among the surfing community, so much so that Tubestation leaders were invited to lead a 'paddle out' for a professional surfer's funeral in which over 100 surfers paddled out to sea on their surfboards while the ashes were scattered in the water.

However not everything has gone smoothly as the work has developed. Tensions between existing church structures and Tubestation mean that dealing with conflict has been part and parcel of the fresh expression's growth. While being extremely grateful for the generosity of the Methodist Church in allowing Tubestation to come into being at all, leaders have grappled with the challenge of allowing new life to emerge without it being 'squashed' by more traditional ways of church working. The pioneering nature of the task is reflected in these challenges but the Tubestation community cite trust and generosity of spirit as being crucial - on both sides - if the challenges are to be successfully met and conflict resolved.

Tubestation was born out of the local Methodist circuit which gave leaders a blank canvas - and freedom - to make the initiative work. The temptation was to set up a church which was totally relevant culturally to surfers, diverging from the local, rather systematic, very traditional way of doing things. However Tubestation's decision to stay in a local circuit means that three years down the line, the community has a very diverse way of expressing its faith. Leaders see it as a very healthy thing, saying it is a united expression rather than an expression which has gone out on a tangent from local traditions.

# Performing

Performing is the aspect of the missional community's life that concentrates on agreeing and then working toward shared goals.

## What can we learn?

Performing centres on the continuous looking forward, looking back, milestone review, planning-not-plans and evaluation processes described in Share *How can we find our way? (Share booklet 05)*. Individuals will perform tasks generated by these processes.

> Michael Moynagh, Andy Freeman
> *Share: How can we find our way* (05)
> Fresh Expressions, 2011
> **Book**

Whether in a tiny or large group, members will require ongoing training and support. Many fresh expressions suffer because missional communities have not taken time to learn from other people.

Learning is at the centre of discipleship. It requires a humble spirit. How much time is your team spending in explicit learning? What does this say about your disposition of heart?

A missional community should consider its initial training needs:

- **learning the principles of birthing and growing a fresh expression;**

    Should members of the team attend a Fresh Expressions *vision day*, short course (*mission shaped intro*) or the one year part-time course (*mission shaped ministry*)?

- **personal evangelism;**

    You might seek advice from the Church Army, for example;

- **where appropriate, health and safety, child protection and the basics of financial management.**

The missional community will need ongoing support:

- **might someone in the community join a learning network and bring insights back to the group?**

    Learning networks enable practitioners to share experiences and wisdom, so as to avoid re-inventing the wheel.

- **might the community benefit from a coach or mentor?**

  Coaching need not always be one-to-one, it can involve whole teams. On-the-job coaching can be a highly effective form of training, though sadly it is not always available.

- **what reading might team members undertake?**
- **how will the community be spiritually nurtured?**
- **how will it remain connected to the wider church?**
- **what prayer support will the community receive?**

The team leader may need support over and above that available to the missional community, such as:

- **a spiritual director or guide;**
- **someone outside the community to cry and laugh with;**
- **practical support (where appropriate);**

  For instance moving house, getting started and finding specialist help;

- **accountability arrangements alongside practical support;**
- **further training in the principles and practice of fresh expressions, or in Biblical studies and theology.**

The leader's and team's spiritual health need particular attention. Some pioneers have been burnt out through the pressure of bringing a fresh expression to birth and team members can be left exhausted. So prioritising the emotional and spiritual well-being of leaders and teams should be a must, however small the new church.

Pioneering teams owe this to themselves, their families and friends, the venture they are leading and above all to God. If a church-start is to be truly the Spirit's work, time spent receiving from the Spirit must be a good investment.

# Adjourning

Adjourning happens if the missional community disbands after a time. Maybe the attempt to start a fresh expression was not successful. Or perhaps the community was fruitful, but for a limited period.

## Facing the truth

In such cases, endings must be take place with dignity. If the missional community can let go, grieve, give thanks for what was, learn and share any lessons, and move on it will enable others in the fresh expression to do the same.

Team members will be helped to let go if they can share their reflections on their journey together and how they feel about the approaching end. Being honest about disappointments and jointly owning the responsibility (not blame) for any short-comings will help to ease the pain.

Mistakes can become a gift to the Kingdom if they can be a source of learning for the wider church. 'These are things that we would have done differently' can be hugely helpful to practitioners who are starting out.

Share your stories
sharetheguide.org/stories

web

When individuals leave the team, remaining members may learn much by asking their departing colleague what they most enjoyed in belonging to the group, have learnt from the experience and what issues the team might give further thought to.

Endings don't have to be loose ends. They can enrich the team and the wider church. In so doing, adjourning - alongside forming, norming, storming and performing - can nurture the leadership potential of the missional community.

> **expressions: making a difference**
> Fresh Expressions, 2011
> Chapter 25: 3:08 @ Kingshill
>
> 3:08 @ Kingshill in Nailsea came to an end after, just two year, but the journey equipped its team for new things.

# 3:08 @ Kingshill

## Story

When a group of people at Christ Church, Nailsea, realised that they weren't reaching families in one of its key areas, they decided to have a go at planting an all-age congregation in Kingshill CofE Primary School. It was easy to reach and attended by the children of many of the families they hoped to reach in that part of north Somerset.

Organisers did some research and opted for a monthly act of worship on a Sunday afternoon after discovering that non-churchgoers described the timings of many church events as 'not particularly helpful'. To avoid Sunday lie-ins, local football and shopping trips, they picked the 'memorable' time of 3:08pm - so 3:08 was born. A small core team leafleted every house in the neighbourhood, advertised in the school notice sheet and local newspaper, and spoke to everyone they met. But despite their efforts, the team never reached the people they really wanted to reach.

On launch day, 43 people turned up, many coming from local churches, but disappointingly there were few genuine newcomers. With hindsight the team felt they did too much 'getting on with it' and not enough thinking and talking about what people really wanted. They learned that if people tell you that a time of worship is not convenient, it does not then automatically mean that that those people would like to go at a different time. 3:08 leaders felt they may jumped to that conclusion a little too quickly.

For one or two people, 3:08 at Kingshill became their spiritual home but the majority of those attending were already churchgoers. After reviewing the progress of 3:08 in its second year, the team unanimously agreed that it should stop but they also felt happy at what had been achieved, enjoyed a celebratory last act of worship at 3:08 - and later discussed how the gifts and skills they had developed might be used in other ways. Many of those skills have now been ploughed back into Christ Church.

Although 3:08 didn't take off there are now two or three developing fresh expressions in the area which are currently working well. Nailsea sees it as a period of constant experiment.

Published 2011 by Fresh Expressions
Registered charity #1080103

Copyright © Fresh Expressions 2011
freshexpressions.org.uk

Fresh Expressions, Athena Drive,
Tachbrook Park, Warwick, CV34 6RQ
0300 365 0563

Authors: Michael Moynagh, Andy Freeman
Series Editor: Karen Carter
Series Designer: Ben Clymo

freshexpressions.org.uk/share/booklets

ISBN 978-0-9568123-7-7

# fresh expressions

## Related resources

**expressions: making a difference**
(Fresh Expressions, 2011)

A DVD containing 28 stories illustrating the lessons to be learnt as fresh expressions of church make a difference to people's lives.

Available from
**freshexpressions.org.uk/shop**

**sharetheguide.org**

An online resource including a guide to fresh expressions, community, blog and learning networks.

**freshexpressions.org.uk**

Further stories and information, plus audio and video material and resources to download and purchase.